S0-APQ-782

Rozanne Travels to Africa to Kiss a Giraffe

By Rozanne Weissman

Bethesda Communications Group

Copyright © Rozanne Weissman 2019

Published by Bethesda Communications Group
4816 Montgomery Lane
Bethesda, MD 20814
www.bcgpub.com

ISBN-13: 978-1-7321501-9-5
ISBN-10: 1-7321501-9-2

PHOTOGRAPHY CREDITS

Photography by author Rozanne Weissman; Orangutan Foundation International; staff at Giraffe Manor, Giraffe Centre, Smithsonian; fellow travelers to Borneo and Africa.

DEDICATION

Dedicated to the wonderful children 👶 & staff at Jubilee JumpStart bilingual infants-pre-K school in Washington, DC where author Rozanne Weissman volunteers.

AUTHOR
Rozanne Weissman

When Rozanne was a little girl, she loved 🖤 her stuffed teddy bear. She loved 💗 watching wild animals at the zoo. **Do you?**

Rozanne was curious about nature—watching plants grow... or a caterpillar 🐛 magically turn into a beautiful butterfly 🦋. *What do YOU love 💕?*

When Rozanne grew up, she created materials for elementary school children—and teacher and parent guides for public broadcasting and others. She involved the nation's teachers and students in Earth Day.

Rozanne worked with Discovery on the launches of its first feature film, *The Leopard Son,* and of its successful Animal Planet channel.

But Rozanne didn't want to just watch animals on TV and movies. She wanted to travel to where animals lived in the wild.

Rozanne's children's book—*Rozanne Travels to Africa to Kiss a Giraffe*—shares her 3 wildlife trips through her still wondrous eyes of a child.

Rozanne LOVES 🩶wild animals—especially mammals. They are most like us.

Like human babies👶, they also drink mama's milk and grow in mama's tummy.

TRIP ONE
What's YOUR Favorite wild animal? Rozanne loves red-haired
orangutans. She wanted to see them "in the wild"—where they live.

She traveled very very far—on many planes ✈ and boats—to the rain forests of Borneo, Indonesia.

Rozanne met baby orangutans whose mommys were in heaven. So they were raised by humans and weren't afraid of people. A baby orangutan put his head in Rozanne's hand & touched her arm.

Orangutan youngsters live with their mamas until age 7 to learn everything to survive.

Without moms, they learn in forest 🧠 school from humans.

A female adult orangutan named Siswi sat next to Rozanne. She ruled Camp Leaky and didn't like other females—orangutan or human.

Eye-to-eye 👁 , nose 👃 -to-nose, the orangutan decided the human woman was no threat to her greater beauty.

TRIP TWO

Where would Rozanne go next to see wild elephants 🐘 and leopards? She went to 5 countries in Southern Africa. She saw herds of elephants, 2 brothers play fighting, lots of little elephants too. But NO elusive (hard to find) leopards...

On a wildlife safari, Rozanne said, "Today, we're going to see leopards." Most people leave Africa and NEVER see elusive leopards. Then a beautiful female leopard crossed right in front of their vehicle!

But it gets better. Rozanne spotted 2 leopard cubs with mama leopard up a tree! Rozanne was the only one on tour to ultimately see 5 leopards. High 5 ✋ Rozanne!

TRIP THREE

Where would Rozanne go next? She never saw
penguins 🐧 in the wild. She wanted to adopt a
baby orphaned elephant 🐘 (no mommy) & kiss a
giraffe. Back to different parts of Africa.

Such cute little South African penguins around
Cape Point on the ocean.

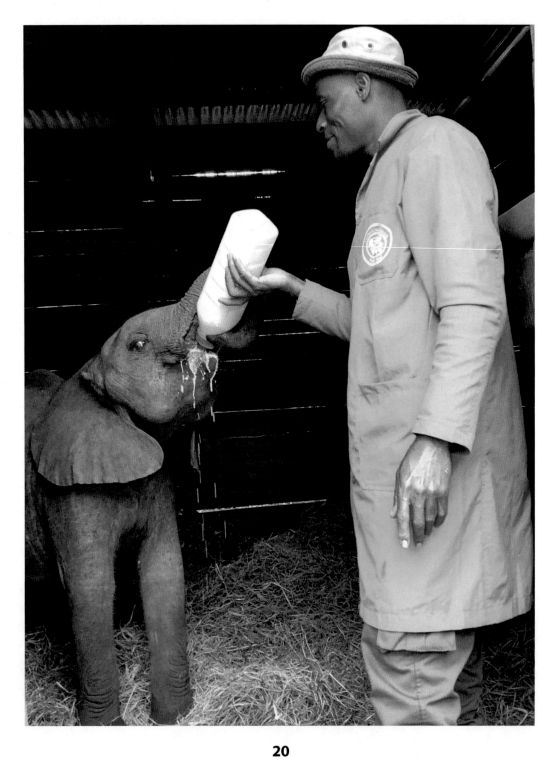

In Kenya, Africa Rozanne fell in love with baby orphaned elephant 🐘 Kiasa. She adopted her. Since she has no mamma, people must help so that she has milk to drink, a keeper to feed her, and a home with other little elephants at the David Sheldrick Wildlife Trust nursery.

Rozanne was scared to actually kiss 😘 a giraffe
🦒. They are Sooooo big!!

Giraffes have very very long necks and VERY BIG HEADS!

And VERY VERY VERY
L-O-N-G tongues. What if a BIG giraffe knocked
her over?

Rozanne had to first feed giraffes pellets that they LOVE by hand. Giraffes stick their heads in the dining room for breakfast at Giraffe Manor. What a funny 😆 sight!

And she went to the wonderful nearby Giraffe Centre to feed more giraffes. Not so hard....

...and then Rozanne built up the courage to kiss 😙 a giraffe! Yay! Another high five 🖐 Rozanne!

THE END

About the Author

A renowned Washington, DC-based marketing communications exec, Rozanne Weissman won more than 60+ national and international awards.

Children, parent, school materials
In her full time jobs as well as for clients of her marketing communications consultancy, Rozanne produced public outreach campaigns and materials for children, parents, and schools.

Her campaigns as an executive for public broadcasting and the Alliance to Save Energy were noteworthy for dramatically expanding the reach and budgets of nonprofits through unexpected, large corporate and nonprofit partnerships.

For her Discovery, Inc. client, Rozanne was instrumental in the highly successful launch and fast expansion of its Animal Planet cable channel that focuses on wild animal documentaries and home pets. She also prepared in-theater materials for children and parents for Discovery's first feature film for theatrical release, The Leopard Son.

Disability dilemma
Jubilee JumpStart bilingual infants-pre-K school asked its volunteer Rozanne Weissman to write a children's book about her three wildlife trips with her photos.

But **how** with permanent hand/wrist disabilities and no computer any longer?

Undeterred, Rozanne dictated this entire book on Seri on a small iPhone 8 screen and laid it out in the SimplePrints app with NO typography choices!

Rozanne's inspirational, book-loving "book consultant" is 3 1/2 years old. She also wants to kiss a giraffe!

Website with leopard print:
http://rozanneweissman.com/

Twitter & Instagram:
@PRlady007

Made in the USA
Monee, IL
23 March 2020

R00024